THE JPS B'NAI MITZVAH TORAH COMMENTARY

Mattot (Numbers 30:2–32:42)
Haftarah (Jeremiah 1:1–2:3)

Rabbi Jeffrey K. Salkin

The Jewish Publication Society · Philadelphia
University of Nebraska Press · Lincoln

INTRODUCTION

News flash: the most important thing about becoming bar or bat mitzvah isn't the party. Nor is it the presents. Nor even being able to celebrate with your family and friends—as wonderful as those things are. Nor is it even standing before the congregation and reading the prayers of the liturgy—as important as that is.

No, the most important thing about becoming bar or bat mitzvah is sharing Torah with the congregation. And why is that? Because of all Jewish skills, that is the most important one.

Here is what is true about rites of passage: you can tell what a culture values by the tasks it asks its young people to perform on their way to maturity. In American culture, you become responsible for driving, responsible for voting, and yes, responsible for drinking responsibly.

In some cultures, the rite of passage toward maturity includes some kind of trial, or a test of strength. Sometimes, it is a kind of "outward bound" camping adventure. Among the Maasai tribe in Africa, it is traditional for a young person to hunt and kill a lion. In some Hispanic cultures, fifteen year-old girls celebrate the *quinceañera*, which marks their entrance into maturity.

What is Judaism's way of marking maturity? It combines both of these rites of passage: *responsibility* and *test*. You show that you are on your way to becoming a *responsible* Jewish adult through a public *test* of strength and knowledge—reading or chanting Torah, and then teaching it to the congregation.

This is the most important Jewish ritual mitzvah (commandment), and that is how you demonstrate that you are, truly, bar or bat mitzvah—old enough to be responsible for the mitzvot.

What Is Torah?

So, what exactly is the Torah? You probably know this already, but let's review.

The Torah (teaching) consists of "the five books of Moses," sometimes also called the *chumash* (from the Hebrew word *chameish*, which means "five"), or, sometimes, the Greek word Pentateuch (which means "the five teachings").

Here are the five books of the Torah, with their common names and their Hebrew names.

> **Genesis (The beginning), which in Hebrew is Bere'shit (from the first words—"When God began to create").** Bere'shit spans the years from Creation to Joseph's death in Egypt. Many of the Bible's best stories are in Genesis: the creation story itself; Adam and Eve in the Garden of Eden; Cain and Abel; Noah and the Flood; and the tales of the Patriarchs and Matriarchs, Abraham, Isaac, Jacob, Sarah, Rebekah, Rachel, and Leah. It also includes one of the greatest pieces of world literature, the story of Joseph, which is actually the oldest complete novel in history, comprising more than one-quarter of all Genesis.

> **Exodus (Getting out), which in Hebrew is Shemot (These are the names).** Exodus begins with the story of the Israelite slavery in Egypt. It then moves to the rise of Moses as a leader, and the Israelites' liberation from slavery. After the Israelites leave Egypt, they experience the miracle of the parting of the Sea of Reeds (or "Red Sea"); the giving of the Ten Commandments at Mount Sinai; the idolatry of the Golden Calf; and the design and construction of the Tabernacle and of the ark for the original tablets of the law, which our ancestors carried with them in the desert. Exodus also includes various ethical and civil laws, such as "You shall not wrong a stranger or oppress him, for you were strangers in the land of Egypt" (22:20).

> **Leviticus (about the Levites), or, in Hebrew, Va-yikra' (And God called).** It goes into great detail about the kinds of sacrifices that the ancient Israelites brought as offerings; the laws of ritual purity; the animals that were permitted and forbidden for eating (the beginnings of the tradition of kashrut, the Jewish dietary laws); the diagnosis of various skin diseases; the ethical laws of holiness; the ritual calendar of the Jewish year; and various agricultural laws concerning the treatment of the Land of Israel. Leviticus is basically the manual of ancient Judaism.

> **Numbers (because the book begins with the census of the Isra-elites), or, in Hebrew, Be-midbar (In the wilderness).** The book describes the forty years of wandering in the wilderness and the various rebellions against Moses. The constant theme: "Egypt wasn't so bad. Maybe we should go back." The greatest rebellion against Moses was the negative reports of the spies about the Land of Israel, which discouraged the Israelites from wanting to move forward into the land. For that reason, the "wilderness generation" must die off before a new generation can come into maturity and finish the journey.

> **Deuteronomy (The repetition of the laws of the Torah), or, in Hebrew, Devarim (The words).** The final book of the Torah is, essentially, Moses's farewell address to the Israelites as they prepare to enter the Land of Israel. Here we find various laws that had been previously taught, though sometimes with different wording. Much of Deuteronomy contains laws that will be important to the Israelites as they enter the Land of Israel—laws concerning the establishment of a monarchy and the ethics of warfare. Perhaps the most famous passage from Deuteronomy contains the *Shema,* the declaration of God's unity and unique-ness, and the *Ve-ahavta,* which follows it. Deuteronomy ends with the death of Moses on Mount Nebo as he looks across the Jordan Valley into the land that he will not enter.

Jews read the Torah in sequence—starting with Bere'shit right af-ter Simchat Torah in the autumn, and then finishing Devarim on the following Simchat Torah. Each Torah portion is called a parashah (di-vision; sometimes called a *sidrah,* a place in the order of the Torah reading). The stories go around in a full circle, reminding us that we can always gain more insights and more wisdom from the Torah. This means that if you don't "get" the meaning this year, don't worry—it will come around again.

And What Else? The Haftarah

We read or chant the Torah from the Torah scroll—the most sacred thing that a Jewish community has in its possession. The Torah is written without vowels, and the ability to read it and chant it is part of the challenge and the test.

But there is more to the synagogue reading. Every Torah reading has an accompanying haftarah reading. Haftarah means "conclusion," because there was once a time when the service actually ended with that reading. Some scholars believe that the reading of the haftarah originated at a time when non-Jewish authorities outlawed the reading of the Torah, and the Jews read the haftarah sections instead. In fact, in some synagogues, young people who become bar or bat mitzvah read very little Torah and instead read the entire haftarah portion.

The haftarah portion comes from the Nevi'im, the prophetic books, which are the second part of the Jewish Bible. It is either read or chanted from a Hebrew Bible, or maybe from a booklet or a photocopy.

The ancient sages chose the haftarah passages because their themes reminded them of the words or stories in the Torah text. Sometimes, they chose *haftarah* with special themes in honor of a festival or an upcoming festival.

Not all books in the prophetic section of the Hebrew Bible consist of prophecy. Several are historical. For example:

The book of Joshua tells the story of the conquest and settlement of Israel.

The book of Judges speaks of the period of early tribal rulers who would rise to power, usually for the purpose of uniting the tribes in war against their enemies. Some of these leaders are famous: Deborah, the great prophetess and military leader, and Samson, the biblical strong man.

The books of Samuel start with Samuel, the last judge, and then move to the creation of the Israelite monarchy under Saul and David (approximately 1000 BCE).

The books of Kings tell of the death of King David, the rise of King Solomon, and how the Israelite kingdom split into the Northern Kingdom of Israel and the Southern Kingdom of Judah (approximately 900 BCE).

And then there are the books of the prophets, those spokesmen for God whose words fired the Jewish conscience. Their names are immortal: Isaiah, Jeremiah, Ezekiel, Amos, Hosea, among others.

Someone once said: "There is no evidence of a biblical prophet ever being invited back a second time for dinner." Why? Because the prophets were tough. They had no patience for injustice, apathy, or hypocrisy. No one escaped their criticisms. Here's what they taught:

> ‣ God commands the Jews to behave decently toward one another. In fact, God cares more about basic ethics and decency than about ritual behavior.
> ‣ God chose the Jews *not* for special privileges, but for special duties to humanity.
> ‣ As bad as the Jews sometimes were, there was always the possibility that they would improve their behavior.
> ‣ As bad as things might be now, it will not always be that way. Someday, there will be universal justice and peace. Human history is moving forward toward an ultimate conclusion that some call the Messianic Age: a time of universal peace and prosperity for the Jewish people and for all the people of the world.

Your Mission—To Teach Torah to the Congregation

On the day when you become bar or bat mitzvah, you will be reading, or chanting, Torah—in Hebrew. You will be reading, or chanting, the haftarah—in Hebrew. That is the major skill that publicly marks the becoming of bar or bat mitzvah. But, perhaps even more important than that, you need to be able to teach something about the Torah portion, and perhaps the haftarah as well.

And that is where this book comes in. It will be a very valuable resource for you, and your family, in the b'nai mitzvah process.

Here is what you will find in it:

> ‣ A brief **summary** of every Torah portion. This is a basic overview of the portion; and, while it might not refer to everything in the Torah portion, it will explain its most important aspects.
> ‣ A list of the **major ideas** in the Torah portion. The purpose: to make the Torah portion real, in ways that we can relate to. Every Torah portion contains unique ideas, and when you put all

of those ideas together, you actually come up with a list of Judaism's most important ideas.

> Two *divrei Torah* ("words of Torah," or "sermonettes") for each portion. These *divrei Torah* explain significant aspects of the Torah portion in accessible, reader-friendly language. Each *devar Torah* contains references to **traditional** Jewish sources (those that were written before the modern era), as well as **modern** sources and quotes. We have searched, far and wide, to find sources that are unusual, interesting, and not just the "same old stuff" that many people already know about the Torah portion. Why did we include these minisermons in the volume? Not because we want you to simply copy those sermons and pass them off as your own (that would be cheating), though you are free to quote from them. We included them so that you can see what is possible—how you can try to make meaning for yourself out of the words of Torah.

> **Connections:** This is perhaps the most valuable part. It's a list of questions that you can ask yourself, or that others might help you think about—any of which can lead to the creation of your *devar Torah*.

Note: you don't have to like everything that's in a particular Torah portion. Some aren't that loveable. Some are hard to understand; some are about religious practices that people today might find confusing, and even offensive; some contain ideas that we might find totally outmoded.

But this doesn't have to get in the way. After all, most kids spend a lot of time thinking about stories that contain ideas that modern people would find totally bizarre. Any good medieval fantasy story falls into that category.

And we also believe that, if you spend just a little bit of time with those texts, you can begin to understand what the author was trying to say.

This volume goes one step further. Sometimes, the haftarah comes off as a second thought, and no one really thinks about it. We have tried to solve that problem by including a **summary** of each haftarah, and then a mini-sermon on the haftarah. This will help you learn how these sacred words are relevant to today's world, and even to your own life.

All Bible quotations come from the NJPS translation, which is found in the many different editions of the JPS TANAKH; in the Conservative movement's *Etz Hayim: Torah and Commentary;* in the Reform movement's *Torah: A Modern Commentary;* and in other Bible commentaries and study guides.

How Do I Write a *Devar Torah?*

It really is easier than it looks.

There are many ways of thinking about the *devar Torah.* It is, of course, a short sermon on the meaning of the Torah (and, perhaps, the haftarah) portion. It might even be helpful to think of the *devar Torah* as a "book report" on the portion itself.

The most important thing you can know about this sacred task is: *Learn* the words. *Love* the words. Teach people what it could mean to *live* the words.

Here's a basic outline for a *devar Torah:*

"My Torah portion is (name of portion) _____,
from the book of _____, chapter
_____.

"In my Torah portion, we learn that_____
(Summary of portion)

"For me, the most important lesson of this Torah portion is (what is the best thing in the portion? Take the portion as a whole; your *devar Torah* does not have to be only, or specifically, on the verses that you are reading).

"As I learned my Torah portion, I found myself wondering:
> *Raise a question that the Torah portion itself raises.*
> *"Pick a fight"* with the portion. Argue with it.
> *Answer a question* that is listed in the "Connections" section of each Torah portion.
> *Suggest a question to your rabbi* that you would want the rabbi to answer in his or her own *devar Torah* or sermon.

"I have lived the values of the Torah by _____
(here, you can talk about how the Torah portion relates to your
own life. If you have done a mitzvah project, you can talk about
that here).

How To Keep It from Being Boring
(and You from Being Bored)

Some people just don't like giving traditional speeches. From our per-
spective, that's really okay. Perhaps you can teach Torah in a different
way—one that makes sense to you.

> Write an "open letter" to one of the characters in your Torah por-
  tion. "Dear Abraham: I hope that your trip to Canaan was not too
  hard . . ." "Dear Moses: Were you afraid when you got the Ten
  Commandments on Mount Sinai? I sure would have been . . ."
> Write a news story about what happens. Imagine yourself to
  be a television or news reporter. "Residents of neighboring cities were horrified yesterday as the wicked cities of Sodom and
  Gomorrah were burned to the ground. Some say that God was
  responsible . . ."
> Write an imaginary interview with a character in your Torah portion.
> Tell the story from the point of view of another character, or a mi-
  nor character, in the story. For instance, tell the story of the Gar-
  den of Eden from the point of view of the serpent. Or the story
  of the Binding of Isaac from the point of view of the ram, which
  was substituted for Isaac as a sacrifice. Or perhaps the story of
  the sale of Joseph from the point of view of his coat, which was
  stripped off him and dipped in a goat's blood.
> Write a poem about your Torah portion.
> Write a song about your Torah portion.
> Write a play about your Torah portion, and have some friends act
  it out with you.
> Create a piece of artwork about your Torah portion.

The bottom line is: Make this a joyful experience. Yes—it could
even be fun.

The Very Last Thing You Need to Know at This Point

The Torah scroll is written without vowels. Why? Don't *sofrim* (Torah scribes) know the vowels?

Of course they do.

So, why do they leave the vowels out?

One reason is that the Torah came into existence at a time when sages were still arguing about the proper vowels, and the proper pronunciation.

But here is another reason: The Torah text, as we have it today, and as it sits in the scroll, is actually *an unfinished work.* Think of it: the words are just sitting there. Because they have no vowels, it is as if they have no voice.

When we read the Torah publicly, we give voice to the ancient words. And when we find meaning in those ancient words, and we talk about those meanings, those words jump to life. They enter our lives. They make our world deeper and better.

Mazal tov to you, and your family. This is your journey toward Jewish maturity. Love it.

THE TORAH

❖ Mattot: Numbers 30:2–32:42

The Torah portion begins with a description of the power of the personal vow and how it must be fulfilled.

The parashah then moves into an account of the Israelites' war against the Midianites. As the Land of Israel is divided among the tribes, the tribes of Reuben and Gad announce that they would rather stay on the other side of the Jordan River rather than entering the land.

Summary

- People must fulfill what they have said that they will do. However, this pertains only to men. If a woman makes a vow, her father or husband has the power to negate it. (30:2–17)
- The Israelites enter into a bloody and merciless war against Midian. Among the victims of battle is Balaam, the soothsayer. The Israelites take captive the Midianite women and children, and they also take the spoil from the battle, for which an inventory is given. Moses gets angry because the Israelites have spared every female. It was the Midianite women, after all, who had induced the Israelite men into paganism and orgies. (31:1–54)
- The tribes of Reuben and Gad ask to be able to settle on the other side of the Jordan River and not enter the Land of Israel. In exchange for the granting of this request, they offer to serve as the shock troops—the advance guard—of the Israelites when they conquer the land. (32:1–42)

The Big Ideas

- **Be careful what you say.** This is a basic Jewish concept, and it is reflected in our religious lives and in our everyday ethics. The word for "word" is *devar,* which is also the word for "thing." A word is a thing, in and of itself. Words, pledges, and vows are so powerful that the most sacred moment of the Jewish year—Kol Nidre on the eve of Yom Kippur, the Day of Atonement—is devoted to annulling vows that we could not realistically fulfill.

- **Not every part of the Torah is nice.** This is a hard truth to accept, especially since we are accustomed to thinking of the Bible as "The Good Book." To be sure, the ancient Israelites did not always act as honorably as we might have wished. Things that would horrify us today, such as a violent war in which women, in particular, are victims, pass almost without comment in the Torah. One of God's greatest gifts to us is the ability to question these texts and to wrestle with their implications.

- **Solidarity with the Jewish people is a crucial part of Jewish life.** The tribes of Reuben and Gad were content to merely live their comfortable lives on the other side of the Jordan River, outside the Land of Israel. Moses had to remind them that the Jews must remain a single, unified people.

Divrei Torah

PUT FIRST THINGS FIRST!

Everyone has had this experience. You are a member of a sports team, or in a school play, or in a choir, or involved in some kind of big group project. Everyone is really engaged in what they are supposed to be doing. But there is always that one kid (if you are lucky, only one) who is, well, a slacker. He or she just isn't giving their all. And, when that happens, the efforts of everyone else suffer. It just isn't fair.

That's sort of what happens in this Torah portion. The tribes of Reuben and Gad ask to be able to settle on the other side of the Jordan River and not enter the Land of Israel proper. When Moses hears this request, he gets very angry and loses his temper (which is standard operating procedure for Moses). "Are your brothers to go to war while you stay here? Why will you turn the minds of the Israelites from crossing into the land that the Lord has given them?" (32:6).

Moses reminds them of how the spies had brought back bad accounts of the Land of Israel. He accuses the people of Reuben and Gad of basically doing the same thing—demoralizing the rest of the Jewish people. Finally, these two tribes offer Moses a consolation prize—that they will act as the shock troops, an elite force, protecting the land from neighboring tribes.

Let's remember that one of the great themes of the book of Numbers is the amount of almost constant complaining that Moses has to endure. There always seems to be a rebellion going on. And now Moses has to deal with yet another, as he comes near the end of his life. It must have stung badly.

And why did it hurt Moses so much? Because it wasn't only that the tribes of Reuben and Gad preferred the land on the other side of the Jordan. It was because they had a lot of cattle, and the grazing land was better there! Here's a great little Hebrew lesson. The word that the Torah uses for "cattle" is *mikneh*—which is related to the word for "buying" and "shopping." In modern terms, the people of Reuben and Gad were simply materialistic.

Look at how those tribes describe what they want to do. "We will build here sheepfolds for our flocks and towns for our children" (32:16). It is distortion of priorities. They put their animals (i.e., their possessions) before their children. Erica Brown teaches: "These people were willing to let go of a sacred, commanded vision to bolster their own material existence while Moses's own sincere appeals to enter the land were rejected." Rashi teaches: "Notice which they mentioned first—they were more concerned about the flocks than about the children."

Several verses later, Moses tells them: "Build towns for your children and sheepfolds for your flocks" (32:24). Moses reminds them of what is really important. It is a message for all of us: first, people, and creating a future for our people; then, and only then, our "stuff."

WAR—WHAT IS IT GOOD FOR?

There's an old classic rock song that goes like this: "War! What is it good for? Absolutely nothing!" Well, not exactly. Sometimes, war is necessary—for example, when you have to defend your people and your land. But, even when that is true, war stinks. It is a tragic, terrible mess.

That might be what bothers you about chapter 31—the account of the war against the Midianites. Why is it even necessary? According to the Torah the Midianite women had seduced Israelite men into orgies and into worshiping their god—part of a concerted effort to destroy the Israelites from within.

And then Moses gets angry because they spared the women! Kill them! Okay, well, you can spare the women who are virgins, but all the other women have to be killed. Oh, and take their stuff. And make a list of everything that you take, just so we get it straight. And, because you have touched corpses, you have to become purified.

What is going on here? To our modern sensibilities this is hard to comprehend and hard to stomach. Does God really command a war of vengeance? Is there such a thing as a holy war? Is it ever permissible to kill civilians?

Let's focus a little bit more closely on this section. God tells Moses to "avenge the Israelite people on the Midianites; then you shall be gathered to your kin" (31:2). How did that feel to Moses? And what's this "then you shall be gathered to your kin" business? Is God saying that this is Moses's final "project"—that once he has performed this act of brutality he can die?

Hold on a second here; this is Midian! The same Midian that Moses fled to, after he killed the taskmaster in Egypt. Midian was where he met his wife, Zipporah, who was, of course, a Midianite woman. Midian was the place where he met his father-in-law, Jethro, who was so kind to Moses and who taught him so much. Sure, the Midianite women did nasty stuff. But the Midianites were also descended from Abraham. They are a "cousin" people to the Israelites.

If this is troubling to you, then it was even more troubling to Moses. In fact, Moses does not go to war against the Midianites himself; he gets others to do it. As a midrash says: "Why did Moses send others to avenge the Midianites, when God told him to do it himself? Because he was highly regarded in the land of Midian, he thought: It is not right for me to cause distress to a people that has been good to me. As the proverb puts it: 'Do not cast a stone in the well from which you have to drink.'"

As contemporary Israeli leader Avraham Burg notes: "In commanding vengeance upon Midian, Moses is essentially destroying a part of himself, of his essence and identity." So is Moses trying to break free from his own Midianite past? Or is he unable to do so and thus has to find others to lead the effort?

It is strange that God chooses this moment to remind Moses that his time is running out: "then you shall be gathered to your kin" (31:2). In fact, there are a few more problems Moses will have to deal with before he dies, and a few more important speeches he will give to the Israelites.

But Moses is being reminded here that his kin are the Israelites, whom he has led for forty years, and who will frustrate him almost to his very final breath. Family is family, for better or for worse. Sometimes we have to do battle for it in ways that are distasteful and tough to do. Yes, we have to choose our battles, and should do so wisely. But there comes a time when we will have to say: this is difficult; this is messy; but this is worth fighting for.

Connections

> Can you give some examples when you have been careful with your use of words, and when you have not been?
> Do you think that it is bad or good to promise (pledge or vow) that we'll do certain things?
> Why did the tribes of Reuben and Gad settle on the other side of the Jordan River? Do you agree with their reasons?
> What are some examples of wars that have been "good"? Wars that have been "bad"? How do we make those kinds of judgments?
> Is it ever good to take revenge on someone?

THE HAFTARAH

❖ Mattot: Jeremiah 1:1–2:3

This is how the book of Jeremiah begins. The prophet experiences two omens: an almond tree and a boiling pot tipping away from the north. In particular, that boiling pot will have major significance. The Babylonians, who will destroy Judah, will be coming from the north, and that "boiling pot" will ultimately not only scald the Jewish people; it will burn them, almost beyond recognition.

Don't look for any deep connection between the Torah portion and the haftarah; there isn't any. In fact, between this week's parashah and the end of the Jewish year, there are few connections between the Torah portions and the *haftarah*. The Jewish calendar now marks one of its most interesting periods: the time before the destruction of the Temple by the Babylonians, beginning after the Fast of the Seventeenth of Tammuz, the breaching of Jerusalem's walls by the Babylonians; the destruction itself (Tisha b'Av), and then seven weeks of consolation for the destruction, leading up to Rosh Hashanah.

This is the first of three prophetic readings of admonition that precede Tisha b'Av. Each one is concerned with the direness of the sins that would lead to destruction. It is as if God is saying: "Don't say I didn't warn you."

A Sort of Love Letter

Have you ever thought of the relationship between God and the Jewish people as a kind of wedding?

When God and the Jewish people first met, it was during the time of the Patriarchs and Matriarchs. From time to time, God would talk to individuals, like Abraham, Sarah, and Jacob. From time to time, they would offer sacrifices to God. No big deal. That was a flirtation.

But then came Sinai. God said to the Israelites: "I am your God." The Israelites said: "We are your people." That was the wedding.

Then came the honeymoon, in which God and Israel wandered together in the wilderness. It was like a young married couple who are trying to figure out what they want to do with their lives and their relationship. And yes, there are bumps in the road—arguing over small things, and even big things. It takes commitment to stick with any marriage.

As we have already seen (in the haftarah for Be-midbar), the marital metaphor isn't all that it's cracked up to be. But Jews still used it to describe the relationship between God and Israel. The sages thought that Song of Songs, the erotic love poetry of the Bible, was actually about the love between God and Israel. That's why the early sage Rabbi Akiva cautions: "Whoever sings the Song of Songs in banqueting houses and turns it into a drinking song loses his portion in the world to come." This is no ordinary "song"; it's about God and the Jewish people.

Watch what happens on Shavuot, the holiday that marks the giving of the Torah at Sinai. It's the wedding itself. Some synagogues actually erect a chuppah on Shavuot. Rabbi David Wolpe teaches: "The Torah is the ketubah [wedding contract] between God and the Jewish people. A ketubah enshrines sacred obligations. Sinai was the chuppah [the wedding canopy], and Shavuot is our anniversary."

And, in fact, when we read the Torah, we are encouraged to read it as if it were a love letter. Rabbi Sue Levi Elwell teaches: "Every year, we reopen the Torah scroll, and week after week, we attempt to discover, decipher and decode the words, as well as the desire behind the words that our ancestors have so lovingly handed down to us." We treat the Torah as we would treat a beloved—caressing her, and carrying her close to the heart.

So, yes, the relationship between God and the Jewish people is like a marriage. It has had good days, and bad days. As Ron Wolfson teaches: "As in all relationships, there is constant renegotiation of the terms of agreement, as well as the terms of endearment." But the most important part of a marriage is devotion.

God is glad that we stuck it out together. That's what God is saying in this haftarah: "You followed Me in the wilderness. Thanks for doing that."

❖ Notes

❖ Notes

CPSIA information can be obtained
at www.ICGtesting.com
Printed in the USA
LVHW032143171118
597514LV00005BA/397/P